Diary of a
Redneck Opera
Zinger

Jay Hunter Morris

DEDICATION

To
My Loves
Meg and Cooper Jack

Table of Contents

ACKNOWLEDGMENTS

My thanks go first to my Mom, Carolyn. That was a tough job you had, and you couldn't' have done it better. Thanks for that.

My Fathers Jack Hunter and Bud. You showed me the power, value, and influence of being a good man.

My sister Kelli, for believing and supporting all these years.

Bill and Dixie Neill, my teachers, my coaches, mentors and most of all, my friends. You always know what I have to work on next.

Most importantly, I express my gratitude to Luiz Gazzola and Opera Lively Press, for that blessed day when out of the blue he called me and proclaimed that he had read my book and wanted to publish it!

Wha wha what?! Listen, I've been writing my Tales from the Operatic Trail for 15 years and their only true purpose was to share my life experiences, lessons, foibles and follies with my friends and family. I confess, I dreamed that one day I might have a hard copy to pass on to Cooper Jack, but after showing my book to several big book mills and receiving negative, or most often no response, I moved on. I mean, I'm a singer, not a writer. Right?

Opera Lively is a young publishing house, sporting two books under their belts to date: *Opera Lively - The Interviews* and the *Opera Lively Guide to Les Troyens*, but I dare say that my *Diary* is at the very least a wacky detour from the Operatic Norm. So in my opinion, Luiz is showing a great deal of courage by taking this chance, giving me this opportunity. He has put in countless hours formatting, organizing, converting, editing, uploading and revising to make this book available, all the while allowing and even encouraging me to keep my voice, my language, my content, bad grammar, spelling and all. I highly doubt that any other publisher would tolerate that, so color me once again, very lucky.

If you are an Opera lover or just Opera curious, please visit Operalively.com and peruse the many forums, articles, and resources that are available. There you will find a list of interviews and candid conversations with MANY of today's most important players in the art form including Joyce DiDonato, Daniele de Niese, Thomas Hampson, Anna Netrebko, Piotr Beczala, Deborah Voigt, Sir John Eliot Gardiner, Juan Diego Flores, and a multitude of others.
Even me.

I've had some champions over the years who saw some potential and kept me alive in this game:
Jonathan, Lotfi, Speight, Ian, Diane, Carol.

Deborah Sanders, you believed when only three of us did. Thanks for aggressively selling me to all who will listen.

Meg is home base. My partner in crime, always entrenched and immovable in my corner.
Thanks for that.

INTRO

So I'm an opera singer. I sing loud and in strange tongues. Russian, German, Czech, French, Italian, Spanish. No, I do not speak these languages fluently, I don't even speak good English. But praise be, I am a good Mimic. And I study a lot. I wear ornate costumes and wigs and makeup and mustachios and capes and big swooshy hats and sometimes I even wear tights... That part I could do without. I fight with swords and knives and guns and I paint and I'm a sailor, a clown, a priest, a poet, a Prince, a thief, and would you believe, an Indian Chief? I am at times mentally challenged, and best of all, I sometimes go insane and kill a few people.

Super Fun! Who's got a great job?

I'm from Paris, Texas. I suspect it would surprise you how many classical musicians hail from the South. I know a lot of us grew up singing and playing in church and I suppose that's where it all started for me. My Father, Jack Hunter, was a Southern Baptist Music Minister. Mother Carolyn, the church organist. My Dad died at the tender age of 41, when I was just 12. But in those few short years he managed to infuse in me a lasting belief that I can achieve anything my heart desires. I like to think that he is very proud to know that I'm out here singing opera. My Mom sure is.

I don't have one of those voices, ya know, where I can just open up and be glorious, but I am stubborn and persistent, and one of these days just maybe I will. I am most certainly not famous, but I've been on stage with a few famous people and I watch them very closely... and I am encouraged, for they are not so different from you and me. They make mistakes, they have bad nights, they get sick and nervous, they have their rituals, their quirks, but with few exceptions, they try really hard to do their best. Sometimes they are amazing. That's the thing; see, they have potential at any given performance or rehearsal to be uniquely excellent. They all bring something different. Me too. Not everybody likes what I do, what I bring, and that's ok, I don't like what I do either sometimes. But 21 years later, I'm still trying.

See, this is really hard, though several members of the Pompous Ass Persuasion are quick to point out that... If Jethro here can do it, anyone can. Haw Haw Haw. Ok, not hard like manual labor hard, but it's hard on your personal life, on your mind and on your spirit. Having people critique you is never fun, in any setting, and certainly not in the world of Classical Music. High Art. It's actually very disturbing, seeing un-niceties about yourself in the paper for all the world to read. But in principle, I try not to put my self-worth up for public debate. My Mom once told me I was just fishin for compliments when I read reviews, so now I don't. I go out there and do my best.

I've learned that for me, there probably won't be some big break, some new production or role or voice lesson or coaching that just brings it all together and everything will suddenly just click, and I'll be a great tenor and in great demand and will possess a flawless technique and I will behave properly and have panache and be clever and artsy and thin and everyone will love me. Not likely. For most of us that just doesn't happen. I just have to do the work. No shortcuts. I have to study hard and practice wisely and passionately, and I should find a very smart agent and let her do all the talking.

Cue Deborah Sanders.

I have a friend who loves to say Life Shows Up. It is his theory that we do our best, hopefully, and life shows up and helps us or teaches us, or challenges us or humbles or uplifts or guides or enables or even kills us. Sounds about right. Life showed up in my favor on so many occasions, in many different forms. I have more than my share of true friends and I have a wonderful family. (That's so much more important than any of this singing stuff). My gratitude and adoration for my wife Meg and son Cooper Jack cannot be translated into a few words, so I best not try. Look at the pictures; you'll see what I mean.

Life showed up and I met Bill and Dixie Neill,

and when I couldn't sing and was completely broke they taught me anyway, with great patience and kindness. And even though they didn't really know me, they invited me into their home and they fed me. I hope that someday I can treat someone with equal compassion. But I kinda doubt it.

I am VERY lucky, blessed if I may, and that's a big part of it, ya know... right place, right time and all that... small town Texas boy out there working with some of the most brilliant musicians in the world. Getting to sing this music with a live orchestra. Ever heard one? It still amazes me, all those sounds, those people coming together.

This operatic career is a dream, with a multisitude of perks. We travel a lot. Up to 10 months a year, great cities of the world most of the time. The FOOD that is out there in the world! The beaches, the views, the history, the undeniable milk of human kindness. I meet people from all over and we usually make nice, forming strange little acquaintances that last only a few weeks. Maybe that's not such a bad thing.

I'm happy to report that so far, I have the best

life of anyone I know. I'm not going to put a CV or Bio in here, but Get This... I got to sing at the Sydney Opera House. I got to study for two years at JUILLIARD. I performed on Broadway in a PLAY. I stood on stage with Kathy Bates. I sang in Nice, in the old opera house that sits right there next to the sea in the South of France. Tokyo, Amsterdam, Paris, Russia, Santiago, Monte-Carlo! I've sung in new operas by Andre Previn, Jake Heggie, John Adams, Elliot Goldenthall, and Howard Shore. This summer I'm singing Captain Ahab in Jake's 'Moby-Dick'. AND, best of all... last year I was the real-life Placido Domingo's understudy. I did all his rehearsals then he came swooping in and sang all the performances and made all the money and it suits me just fine. I am proud to hold that man's coat.

See, I told you I was blessed.

And yet, believe it or not, sometimes I want to quit. Because I miss home or the grass is greener or I'm sick of unfitted hotel sheets and order-out food and I'm tired of staring at train schedules in chicken scratch and I'd rather be sitting on my own couch watching my baby boy grow... but then the thought of getting a real job settles in. I wouldn't know where to start.

So I count my many blessings, and know that no matter where I go or what I do, my Momma's favorite performance will always be the ones at the First Baptist Church in Paris, TX. Singing the songs my Daddy taught me.

The older I get, the more I understand her position.

Now behave,

JMo

HIPPIES

2001

Ya know what I love about California? The
girls, of course. And the Hippies. I don't
know, I just love the word and the distaste it
so quickly conjures. Hippies, all peace and
love and flower power and one with nature
and the universe and philosophical and
healthy and dirty and just all evolved and open
and kind and stinky.

I've had more than a few encounters with
Hippies, mostly because my girlfriend Jill
wishes she were a Hippie. Oh yeah, back
when we were first dating and ya know, all
open and willing and trying to please each
other and show how pliable and elastic we

were as human beings and stuff like that. Come on, you remember when it was like that.

For example, a few years back when I was singing my very first Wagnerian role, Walter von Stolzing in *Die Meistersinger*, right here in San Francisco. Jill was coming out for a visit and one of her Hippie friends, I think it was her masseuse, told her about this retreat, this Healing Center that we just had to go visit.

Just terrific.

It's up in California's Napa Valley, just north of Calistoga. Jill produced lovely brochures full of scenic mountains and streams and log cabins and warm natural springs just bubblin over with healing hooky pooky. She suggested we sign up for a cleansing weekend where we would take some form of herbal wire wisk broom to our innards and clean us out but good. Probably do a bit of spiritual housekeeping as well. We shall eat nothing but fruit and couscous and tabuli and tofu and granola and yogurt and we shall take yoga and guided meditations and commune with Mother Nature as well as the God inside each and every one of us and we shall have massage for both the mind and the spirit and we shall by golly leave this establishment one outstanding young American hippie.

The obvious truth is, if she had asked me to run across the rodeo fair grounds in just my boots and a smile, I'd a probably done it. My biggest concern was that everybody at this place was gonna be running around butt nekid and from what I've seen on HBO, these nudie places seem to only feature Bad Nekid.

But being all evolved and open and worldly myself, she easily strong-armed me into it. Booked a whole weekend of this nonsense. We check in at the gate and get quite the disapproving gaze from a fella in a long scraggly beard wearing a dusty bed sheet mumbling something against the leather seats in my foreign rental car.

I asked him if he had corn for breakfast this morning and pointed at his beard.

He said, 'I don't remember eating any corn,' and I burst out laughin and spilt my Dr Pepper everywhere.

Before we even make it into camp, this

Elderly woman, very elderly, came running down the hill squealin or singin with glee just as nekid as could be. Grinnin ear to ear, gigglin all the way. I did not need to see that. I turned to Jill and said, 'What have you done?'

We're booked, we paid for it, we're goin in. We pull into camp and sure enough there's about 200 Hippies all runnin around nekid. Kids and pets too. Sittin there having a picnic, eating pomegranates and nuts, kickin the hacky sacky and playin the guitar and the flute and tambourine and the bongos. I'm pretty sure I hear a lute. They're swimming and sunning and napping and for heaven's sake I think those two over there are headed towards some form of fornification. Haven't even unpacked my bags yet.

So you get the picture. The food was awful; whatever that green algae poo they made me drink just gave me the worst gut rot ever, which I was banished to endure in an open-air, no stall, unisexual outhouse for the love of all decency!

They had this hot spring, which they called the Quiet Pool. I called it the cesspool. The steaming, murky water smelled of spoilt cantaloupe or cabbage, first off. But what really bugged me was the fact that it was just stuffed poppin full of Hippies. They're in the cesspool up to their nostrils, sitting there lookin all serene. I just wanted to smack em. I did not want to go in there, but Jill just beat me down. We drove out here, we paid for it, just man up and drop your drawers and get in that nasty hot water with all those nekid Hippies.

She's dragging me towards it like I'm an ornery child. I'm whimperin. Then the Gawds intervened and right there in front of us this tall, saggy, skinny Hippie walks into that Quiet Pool with big ole red sores that looked kinda like twizzlers all over his flappy behind.

Whiew, that was close.

We giggled all the way to our sorry little room, then spent the night hoping that the morning yoga and yogurt and mountain hike might somehow dislodge that image. Course we couldn't sleep, 'cause you know what all those folk were doing? They were having relations. And they do not care, they whoop it up for all the world to hear, right down there in that big meditation center just below. Well, it's only natural and all God's creatures do it and the rest of that uppity hoo-hah, but I'd like the option to not hear it.

I had my granola and algae poo the next morning, went on a hike that just frustrated me senseless because about every thirty feet we ran into another hippie that wanted to stop and share with us all about his inner peace and tranquility and of course, inquire about our own. I was holdin on because I had a massage that afternoon, and I just knew that would relieve me of all my emotional and physical turmoil. I mean, it's pretty hard to screw up lying there getting yourself all greased up and rubbed on, right?

Right.

Her name was Wendy. She was pretty in that tall, skinny, frilly, Renaissance, musty kinda way. There was a solitary hand towel on the massage table that I was to somehow fit under. She had on the fruity music and candles and burning aromatherapy and crickets and frogs and bubblin water and pan flutes. About 45 minutes into it I'm starting to give in, just calm down, seek my inner child and guardian angel and all that... and she farted. Wendy did. Not a short, accidental slippage, but a long, slow, intentional one. She enjoyed it.

Then she said, 'Pardon me.'

What really pissed me off was that undertone of everyone does it, it's a natural body function and if you have a problem with it then you are just childish and not nearly as evolved as I am.

I started laughin. Couldn't stop. She became annoyed and petulant and left in a huff.

I told the spa manager I wasn't gonna pay for 90 minutes, I only got 45. He asked what the problem was and in front of everybody I proudly declared...

'Wendy farted.'

I hate Hippies.

SAFEWAY

2004

I got in a fight today. In the Cheeps and
Deeps department of the Safeway. An honest
to goodness scrapin scratchin cursin kickin
hair pullin name callin fourth grade
playground testing of ye ole cahones. And not
just any Safeway either my friend. The Marina
Safeway here in lovely San Francisco. This
Safeway is rumored to be the premiere pickup joint for the young, the hip, the talented,
athletic, successful, beautiful nouveau riche
heterosexuals of this fine city. I live one block
away and I have never seen any persuasive
evidence supporting this. And tho I am
unattached and extremely available these days
I've never talked to one single girl in the three
months I've been here and not a one of them

has talked to me. And ya know I'm very European in my shopping habits, I'm in there at least once a day. Just in case.

I'm mindin my own business, ya know, choosing just the right Crunchy Cheetos to accompany my P, B & J and this guy says… 'Ya know, I'm getting sick of this.'

I looks up, bristling at the unsavory condescension in his whiny tone, but he's not talkin to me. He's talkin to his girlfriend. Elise. She reminds me of a cute wittle bunny wabbit. With a voice flooded with innocence and naïveté she coos, 'What exactly is it that you are sick of… Remy?'

His name is Remy. And she's a cutie all righty. Upon closer inspection Mr. Grumpy Pants here looks like a sanctimonious little weasel in his pressed blue jeans, loafers, and pink polo schweater. He's about 5 ft 6 inches tall, and I'm guessin he weighs 130 lbs soppin wet. I'm thinking, why I oughta whoop yer skinny little ass, talkin to this sweet girl like that. He's got this itty bitty mouth all puckered up in contempt and he spits 'You know very well what I am sick of Elise, and frankly, I'm growing a bit weary of your attitude.'

His eyes look like they're about to pop right out of his head and his face is all red and scrunched up and she looked at me and I saw great sorrow in those eyes. Here she was, just pickin out some Sun Chips, and Remy is throwing another of his tantrums. She was mortified and humiliated and I tell ya, I could hear her silently crying out to me for help. So I walked toward her, slowly, oozing enormous oodles of confidence and manliness, and a Mexican guitar band started playing foreboding strains and we never broke eye contact as I said softly... 'Just walk away, shame on him.'

And Remy barked... 'Shame on you Sasquatch! Go eat your Cheetos and milk you little girl.'

My eyes remained on hers as I smiled and said... 'Feisty little fella, ain't he?'

I was chuckling out loud, quite pleased with myself when he jumped up and slapped me on the side of my head. Really hard. This little varmint just slapped me on my head in the Marina Safeway!

'Remy, you're a poop stain on the fabric of

her life and if you don't mind your manners I'm gonna...'

And he lunged at me swingin and kickin and scratchin and shovin and flailin like some spoilt little brat and he knocked me backwards and I tripped into my basket stepping right on the Wonder bread. Then I took down two shelves of Tostitos and about a dozen glass jars of Queso and Guacamole. I tries to get up but I'm slippin in the muck as I plant the heel of my hand on a large shard of cheesy glass. Ouch. And he's standing over me, taunting me. Remy is like this rabid little dog, like a Chihuahua on crack and I can't even understand a word he's sayin and I really am gonna whoop his skinny little ass if I could only get up and Elise is yelling at me, at moi, 'Leave him alone! Why don't you just mind your own business asshole!'

Huh? She's yellin at me?

An unusually fit supermarket security guard is running our way and he's got all his gear on and he's talking into a headpiece sayin 'we got us some domestic violence on aisle 13,' he needs backup.

I gotta get to Remy and land a blow or two or my life here is over. Every passer-by at the Marina Safeway will snicker and whisper 'that's the big Opera Sissy, got his butt whipped by a coked up weenie dog and a bunny wabbit.'

I'm slippin and sliddin and scramblin to get up and he's still barkin at me so I grab a can of Frito Bean Dip and fastball it to him sqwah in the nets. Now he's not so tough, squeelin and whimperin. I finally got to my feet, ready to recapture my manhood when Darren, the security guard at the Safeway tackles me from the blind side. I mean, he full-on tackles me and sends me flyin back into the Cheeps and Deep. Seems that all he saw was the girl screamin at me. And then, ya know, the tossing of the bean dip. This latest tumble sent a piece of glass thru my shorts and into my right butt cheek. Super.

Another guard arrives and they subdue me. One minute I'm out shopping peacefully, and in the blink of an eye I've got two grown men on top of me, telling me to 'Calm down Sir,' pressing me face first into cheesy glassy guacamoley.

A report was filed as the good patrons of Safeway stared and pointed. I saw one guy with a video camera, and he told me to check out his blog tonight, he got it all right there on tape. The pharmacist thinks I should go to an ER and get a tetanus shot.
Yeah, that'll be fun.

Remy is undecided as to whether or not he will press charges... but his nets, Elise assures me, are just huge. So the police did come and take our statements. Just in case.

I explain to Barney Fife that I am indeed a very sophisticated and distinguished opera star in town performing in the World Premiere of *Doctor Atomic.*

"Never heard of it", says he.

He wants my autograph right there at the bottom of his report.

Remy proclaims, "Hey Mr. Opera Star, your butt's bleeding all over the floor."

He and Elise giggle and snuggle and exit hand in hand.

Oh the indignity! The Shame!

AND, today was my birthday.

Just terrific.

OUEST

2000

You guys, I just had the greatest night ever!! Do you know John Lithgow? The guy from *Third Rock from the Sun? Terms of Endearment? Garp? Shrek, Cliffhanger,* and best of all... *Footloose!* The small town minister, the No Dancin in my town Preacher Man? I love him, he has been my favorite actor for years, mostly because he just seems like a good guy, ya know? The Epitome of Versatility. Light on the Posing and Ego and Glam and Actor Speak.

Well it just so happens my girlfriend Jill is doing a new Broadway musical with him called "The Sweet Smell of My Ass". I mean

"Sweet Smell of Success". They're rehearsing now and open in a few weeks.

So, she got an invite to a special, newly released screening of "All That Jazz", at the Museum of Modern Art, here in NYC. I'm happily riding her coat tails and meet her after rehearsal, and well, it turns out John is going too. Because he was in it!

He asked if we wanted to ride with him. In his Limo. YEAH! I WANNA RIDE IN YOUR LIMO! I yelped like a giddy leetle girl. And we rode in his limo, and we're a bit early, so we went over to this schmantzy bar at the Peninsula Hotel and had cocktails before and...

Oh... Yes, Mr. Lithgow, right this way, and here, let me take your coats and here's our finest wine, and your money's no good heah and oh, they are with you so they must be very important as well, and faw faw faw, and then we went in for the showing and cameras flashing and over here for a photo op and oh, here's Roy Scheider and Ben Vereen and can we take more pictures and then we skirted away, and I shouted back at the photogs in my horrid British Accent... 'No More Pictures!

Cahn't you peeple just leave me Ahloone?!'
No one laughed. Except John.

Then we're back in the limo and John asks if
we wanna go to dinner with him... YEAH!
WE WANNA GO TO DINNER WITH
YOU! And he took us to Ouest, this super
cool new hip nine-week waiting list restaurant
and we walked right in, and I told the Maitre
Di that it was a styupid way to spell West, and
he retorts in a most snooty French accent, and
then he sees John and... Oh la la, right dees
way, and the best table and fancy foods and
fishy things and tiny portions and Martini's
and Wine and three green beans and desserts
on the house and everyone buzzing and
staring and ga ga. Jill and I and John Lithgow.

Now, I happened to be on the program with
him at a Kennedy Center Concert last year,
and in secret I was hoping he would say 'Oh
Yes, I remember you, and aren't you
mahvelous.' But he didn't. Wah. Still, I think
he was probably under the impression that
I'm not a Moron and I didn't sit there with my
bladder stretched to about forty times capacity
the whole night because I didn't want to miss
anything. Or that I wasn't fighting the urge to
shout out 'I'm having dinner with...' ya know,

and be an idiot... but I gotta tell ya, I really wanted to. I wanted to gush, to be a really big fan.

Especially when the night came to a close. Not because he's a movie star, but because he was smart and kind and funny and he looked me in the eye and he listened to my silly stories and gave me courtesy laughs. He treated Jill like she was his favorite leading lady, not a dancer he just met. He favors the stagehand with the same kindness and respect as the composer. He writes children's books and teaches them about music and he knows opera and is very well read and even in all the hoopla, he's been married for 20 years to a History Professor at UCLA. And he lit up the room when he spoke of her. His son is going to study Jazz Bass at NYU, and John is so proud.

On the way out, at midnight, he stopped and spoke to all of those sloppy drunk people at the bar who couldn't get tables, the ones who shouted out... 'Hey aren't you...' I pretended to be his bodyguard and he smiled and shook their hands and was patient and gracious, more gracious than I often am with my own friends.

Look, I know it is terribly unattractive to be so Star Struck, but the point is that we hope that there are people out there who are intelligent and charismatic and successful and maybe even big time movie stars, that are just like you and me, or even better, and I'm here to tell ya, there are.

John Lithgow for one.

WAHOOO

2006

... Not exactly what ya wanna hear 20 miles from shore in the Gulf of Mexico.

Twas a fine day, December 15, in Venice, Louisiana. A cloudless sky sparkles on calm, one-foot seas. Good friends, a freezer full of soda pop, two enormous bags of PopEye's Fried chicken, and the promise of large fish. Yellowfin Tuna, Amber Jack, Marlin, dare we, even a Wahoo?

Paul, John and Jim have a glorious spankin new fishing vessel, a 35-foot, three out-board Mercury with all the bells and whistles. Course it's not running. Someone, in an ill-fated attempt to change a spark plug, stripped that rascal but good, and now the manifold must be replaced. Man, I'm glad I didn't do that. So, here we are, the best fishin day of the season and the new boat is ashore in a shop.

But we shall not be defeated! Nay, we shall charter another boat for an enormous sum of money and we shall laugh and sing and frolic in the sun whilst someone else does all the work and we shall venture forth and claim the bounty that the sea will surely give. Especially since we're paying so handsomely for it.

We gather at the Ass Crack of dawn, me and Paul and John and Angele and Bryn. And Kip, our Good Capitan. Skipper Kipper. We load the supplies and head down the Mississippi towards the Gulf of Mexico. Not far tho, because one of the two engines runnith not. We turn back, and Skipper Kipper secures us another, even larger bateau. That's Cajun for big boat, methinks. This one here has a cabin up front where I can sleep, so I'm pleased as peach punch.

Boat #3, off we go! Optimism abounds! Neptune will certainly smile on our unbridled enthusiasm! The first catch of the day... a rare Wahoo! A Trophy fish! Quite possibly the largest one landed this year. I wrestled that beast for near 30 minutes, the fastest fish in the sea, rumored to swim up to 60 MPH. All right, Bryn caught it. Six feet long, 84 pounds with a needle nose head and rows of short, razor-sharp teeth. I fought a Baby 10-pound Blackfin Tuna for 20 minutes and pulled a hammy in the process.

Anyhoo, Wahoo, it's gettin on about 5pm and with our bellies full and spirits exhausted, we turn North, home, shore. Just as we are lulled into a fine nap by the slapping of waves and the rocking of boat and the humming of motors an acrid odor tickles the nose. Before we can ask, ummm, is that smoke...? A beep starts a-beepin.

Skipper Kipper, what's going on? He scurries about for a bit, then stands, frozen, his eyes locked on the black smoke billowing behind the ship.

Wha wha what?! We all look to the engine, and there too, billowith black smoke.

Our fearless leader Skipper Kipper succumbs to a moment of panic and screams... 'Get the Life Jackets, the Boat's on fire!' Not exactly

what ya wanna hear... We looked at each other, almost laughed, gazed about in all directions at nothing but sea, then scurried after the floaties. Yer Jokin. Surely we're not jumpin in this ocean 20 miles from shore. Paulie mans the mike and starts singing "Mayday, Mayday, the boat's on fire!"
John, Bryn, Angele and the good Skipper Kipper all showed remarkable composure and doused out the flames while I stood whimperin in the corner, ready to jump.

The one hour ride to shore took six. We sputtered in on about 1/4 of an engine. Might as well have been paddling.

Back at the Marina we grilled the Wahoo, and I'm tellin ya, nothing ever tasted finer. Tho we never really feared for our lives, it rattled the cage pretty good... what's really important and all that.

I'm thinking I oughta take up a new hobby - chess, no, too hard... checkers or cards or baking or knitting, something... safe.

And dry.

Jay, Angele and John Crawford, Bryn Terfel
and Paul Groves

DOLLY

2006

Last year my friend Terrilyn lost her mind and purchased a car over the internet from some woman named Inez in Ohio, sight unseen, except for those pix on Auto Trader or Cars-R-Us or E-bay or some such. Inez says she drove it down to the village once a week for the last 30 years.

Hippie.

It's a sassy little thang, a 1976 Citroen Dolly Convertible. Red and white with a ragtop. Actually, it's more like a sheet of red seran wrap held in place with toothpicks. Super safe. It's made by the Frenchies and I just don't see what good could ever come from it.

They can make some pastries now, some foie gras and some fine wine, you betcha, but cars? Methinks not.

Dolly's been sitting in the barn behind Terrilyn and Hugh's house gathering fleas and wasps and hornet nests and fire ants and ticks and other biting, itching insecti ever since. Terrilyn has never driven it. But she did remember to leave the windows down so that all manner of critter and vermin and varmint might go wee wee and poopies on the seats as they please. Jimmy Hendrix the cat has put an empty bird nest in the backseat, and it looks and smells like Dolly has doubled as zoo and porta-potty for just about eight months.

So I bought it.

Well I figured it's kinda cool and sporty in that impoverished, gnatty, Euro, musty old vintage sorta way. I most certainly did not buy it with the foolish notion that it might be a chick magnet. Learned that lesson from Paulie... his 1963 Corvette Sting Ray proved to be a frumpy, lonely, middle-aged giggling man magnet, so I have no delusions about such things.
I am pleased to report that she's very fuel

efficient and environmentally friendly. She's only got two cylinders and like half a tiny horsepower. What is that anyway, horsepower in an automobile? I spent three years of my youth working at Chief Auto Parts for a one-armed redneck named Cooter Collins, but I could never understand why we need to bring horses into the equation.

Whatever. Dolly's got 7 or 8 geriatric Chihuahuas under the hood. And, oh yeah, she's got no AC. No air-conditioning in Dallas, where it's 112 degrees every single day all summer long.

In spite of the fact that this will clearly end badly, I was just tickled to death to go pick up my new project and take her home. This is gonna be fun, right? Give her a little TLC and she'll be fine. I brushed away the spider webs and dirt dobbers, the most evident trespassers. Told em to git.

You understand, this is a very small car. The first time I saw it I just knew 30 clowns were about to climb out honking horns and throwing confetti. I get in and Hugh Charles and Jeffrey have a good belly laugh, pointing out the fact that I look like ten pounds of feed in a five-pound bag.

Not very friendly.

Screw you guys, I'm goin home.

Dolly runs great. Seriously. A little anemic perhaps, out on the highway with all those big rigs and SUV's blowing by, but she can sustain 70 kilometers per hour. I have no idea how to convert that, but going by the feel factor I reckon that's about as fast as that go-cart I built in the 7th grade. Rides about as smooth too.

So off I go, not far tho, cuz I'm starvin and there's a Chick-fil-A right on the corner with my name on it. I pull up to the drive thru window... the young lady is all agaah and agooo at me in my sporty little car and I'm trying to get my money out and there's just not a lot of negotiating room here, so I'm leanin back, pushin back on the seat tryin to lift up my behind so I can get my hand in my pocket at this impossible angle and I pushed too hard and the seat broke. It actually snapped out of the tracks that held it in place, so I go flying back... kinda like a rocking chair tipping over backwards... and my left leg of course went with me and popped the clutch and Dolly blasted a shotgun back-fire and the car lurched forward about 15 feet and sputtered and died.

Scared that poor girl holdin out my sandwich half naked. She dropped my strawberry milk shake right there on that hot driveway. If that weren't bad enough the ding dong in the Escalade behind me with the phone to her head doesn't seem to notice and just pulls right up and takes my spot at the window.

Anyway, I can't fix the seat and I can't go back to Hugh Charles for help, I just left there ten minutes ago. So I hit the highway, 5 o'clock pm, rush hour, 112 degrees, trying desperately not to tip over backwards and kill myself dead.

Even tho my pokiness almost caused a handful of fatal accidents, I am pleased to report that I have never felt so unconditionally embraced and adored by humankind. People love me. I mean the car. They smiled and waved and gave me thumbs up and the okie dokey sign and honked and some of them young ones even had their camera phones out taking pictures on the freeway. It's true. I smile and give courtesy waves, if I can be bothered.

Before I hit the downtown traffic I figured I'd pull off and take the scenic route. At the first stoplight Dolly stalled. I don't really know if any of the lights or blinkers on this thing even work. Now the horns are honkin and I've no horn with which to honk back. All I can do is hang my hound dawg head in shame while Dolly goes... rehr rihr rahr rahr, rehr rihr rahr rahr... over and over again.

I'm schweatin. Hand signals and gestures abound. The same people who loved me so just moments ago are now cursing my very name. And my legs are itchin.

Every time I had to stop, the car died and required an eternity to crank up again.
It took me one hour and twenty minutes to travel two miles on Mockingbird Lane.

My arms are itchin. I look over at the white Chick-fil-A bag on the seat next to me and I see a tiny critter havin a snack. Is that an ant?

'Scram!' Says I. 'I'm trying to start this French car!'

I stare in absolute horror as about ten chiggers or fleas or ticks or some such frolic joyfully amongst the hairs on my arm. They got themselves a little circus going here. I started flailin on myself, brushin and scratchin and slappin and thrashin about, squeelin like a wee little girl.

Upon close inspection, it's over folks, they are everywhere. My shorts, my shirt, my back's itchin... God Help me!! I'm infested! What am I to do, bring em all into my home? Stop by the firehouse and have em hose me down? Go to the Pet Smart and get myself dipped?

Why won't this car start?! Please, Oh God...

Soppin wet with summer sweat and scratchin and traumatized and just darn near hyperventilating with stress, I finally make it home.

Now stay with me, picture this... I have an underground parking garage with a remote controlled door. The gate starts to go up, but Dolly has died again, she's not startin, and now the door is coming down.
I decided to push her over the lip and down the steep incline, which by the by, dead ends

in a sharp left turn at the bottom. I get her rolling and try to jump in. She's picking up pace, I'm doing the left legged pogo hop and every time I try to jump in my booty hits the steering wheel. Not much room here, the seat's still askew. Access denied. Hop. Nope. Hop. Denied. Can ya see it?

Anyway I finally got about half in when I remembered that Dolly has no power steering, no power brakes, and I'm barreling down a parking ramp towards a curb and two cement pillars. Ya gotta turn left. The tiny tires are squealing and I'm squealing and I turn the wheel hard and stomp on the brake and my seat flips all the way into the back, and by the hair of both my Chinny Chin Chins, I just do avoid those concrete pillars. But not the curb. Blew out the right front tire.

For sale

COCKATOO

2005

Some of you might remember the episode with my black dress pants... opening night in Seattle, the little old Chinese tailors? I know I told some of you. The pants were too small and I begged the sweet old Chinese couple to let them out all the way and when I picked them up she yelled at me... 'You no ret aw pan no mo! Deez nice pan! You nee go on dieh! No Mo Loom!'

And I'm like, well, yeah, I know, thanks for that. Anyway, I haven't worn deez nice pan since. Till last Saturday nite. I took them off the hanger about an hour before the downbeat of *Carmen*. Twas a concert version of sorts with the Dallas Symphony in Vail, Colorado. Rocky Mountains in the summer time, tough gig. So my stomach squiggled as I pondered the possibility that once again deez nice pan may not comfortably contain my hearty physique. Why on earth didn't I just try them on about a week ago? Deep breath, and glory be they fid dit and the angels sang and the Earth rejoiced, I'm telling ya the very trees of the field clapped their hands. Dodged another bullet. Sorta.

I did all right I guess, ya know in the concert, all the way up till that very last page. At this point, the fella I'm portraying, Jose, I know, I look just like a Jose... well, Don Jose has had just about enough of this Carmen and her gypsified ways so I pull out my knife and stab her right when that orchestra swells and gets all violent and angry. That'll teach her. And as I'm laying the Gypsy down gently onto the stage floor, with me arse regrettably pointing directly at the good folk of Colorado, the seat of my pants sang out... CCGGggrrrriiip!

The conductor winced, Carmen giggled, and in my peripheral vision I catch the here-to-fore half asleep patrons nudging and snickering, pointing and chuckling at my misfortune. No mo loom. I whispered to Carmen, thank goodness for black under-britches, and I stood up and sang the last line and did my best to be all dramatical and emotional and such. I skulk to my dressing room and there in the mirror I see that my black under-britches are indeed not showing, just the white tuxedo shirt tucked into deez nice pan. I've got a little white cotton bunny tail. Upon my exit I'm greeted by about thrice as many well wishers as ever, tho not with praise and adoration, but cackles, chuckles, cajoles and cracks. One fella from Texas asked if he could take a photograph with my backside. Sure, why not. They just can't wait to tell all their friends. I've GOT to get a new suit. No mo Loom.

Anyway, that's not the point of this here story, I just wanted to set the mood, let you in on my state of mind. The next day I packed my bags and crawled thru construction traffic all the way to Denver. And ya know what? When they finally opened all four lanes instead of just that one, and by the by, I never saw one person, not one vehicle, not a wreck, not a can of paint, not a broom, I mean absolutely no work being done for about 45 miles, well here stands a man waving an orange flag and holding a sign that said Speed Up. I swear I almost pulled over and killed him dead.

Instead I rolled my eyes at him, flew to Dallas, and drove joyfully from the airport to my new abode.

In case you don't know, I am no longer homeless. Got myself a loft in Dallas, so, thank you to all my wonderful, multitude of friends who shared their homes and couches and patience and snacks with me for what must have felt like about twenty years. I LOVE my new place. Y'all come on over. We can sit out on the terrace and throw frozen grapes at those skinny little trendy 20-somethings down there shopping at Urban Outfitters. It's fun.

So, on my way home from the airport I stopped at Grandy's and got myself some double Chicken Fried Steak and taters and I'm hauling it and my luggage into my new lair and I step off the elevator and there stands this woman. Don't know her. She seems to be a grown up, somewhere between 30 and 50, and she's kinda creepy lookin and she says she needs some help. The electricity is off in her apartment and she needs to use my phone, which is buried in my fully stuffed duffle bag and she is going on and on about her crisis which I'm not the least bit interested in and I finally interrupt her and say all right all right, come on in you can use my phone.

She's calling the building manager at 10:30 pm, and proceeds to leave a lengthy, somewhat frantic message. I futz about, putting things away, setting out a plate and fork and napkin, she's still prattling on and so I go upstairs and I'm unpacking and ya know all I want is to sit down on my couch and tune in some mindless riff-raff on the tele and enjoy my Southern fried everything but this odd woman is still in my kitchen on my phone!

At long last there is silence and I'm thinking surely she's gone, but when I sneak a peek over the balcony she's still standing down there staring into the abyss. I wave and say, 'all righty then, good nite and good luck... nitey nite.'

Uh oh, she's whimpering. And not moving. Not fair. So, I go down the stairs and gently ask what the matter is. Big mistake, cuz she starts off on this tirade about injustice and electric companies and red tape and mismanagement and she can't see a thing in her apartment and the worst day of her life and they left her a key to another unit so she can store her perishables but she doesn't know which number and I'm thinking my dinner's getting cold, please go away. Scram. She asks for a candle and I give her a flashlight and think surely this is the end of it.

Shiew... go home. Right? Nope, there's more. I tuned out most of it but I did zero in on one thing... she wants to put something in my freezer. I said, huh? She explains that this is so very important to her, a matter of life and death and that if it should thaw out and spoil she would just have to fall on her sword.

I say very slowly... 'What? What do you want to put in my freezer?'

'A biological sample,' says she.

I'm thinking, germ warfare? Toxins? Something really stinky? Who is this woman? She's creepin me right out, and so I have a little closer look and she's got these wild, red, panicky eyes and she's suffering from years of poor hygiene. She's talking too fast and looking too nutty and so I say...

'All right, hold on now, I let you use my

phone, but what is it exactly that you want to put in my freezer? And surely you have another option, a friend perhaps, anyone else in this town besides a bedraggled, hungry, grumpy stranger? Don't ya?'

Now she's really crying. She tells me it is a very important cryogenically frozen biological sample. Austin Powers comes to mind. It's a pet sample. I'm like, 'you wanna put half-frozen dog poop in my freezer?'

She says she doesn't care for dogs. It's from her pet bird, Tui. I giggled. Yer kiddin.

No, she kiddith not, in fact it is her bird, not a sample, a dead bird. She explains that some years ago her beloved Cockatoo, Tui... which I'm thinking is that colorful tropical bird named Toucan Sam on the kids cereal box, well Tui was wrongfully murdered by harmful pesticides or fertilizers or some such. Been frozen in her freezer ever since.

A little therapy is clearly in order.

Surely I'm getting punked or pranked or crank yanked, I mean this is crazy. But she's a woman in distress and I finally just said fine, bring it on down. Nothing much in my freezer anyway. No, she needs me to come with her, she's scairt of the dark. And it's heavy. Her cryogenically, hermetically frozen very dead bird Tui.

She opened the door to her freezer and it did not look good. Didn't look cold and there were puddles of water and something did not smell pretty in there. She pulled out this stainless steel canister and the thing is way way bigger than I expected and she handed it to me and I said...

'This isn't even cold, how long has the power been off?'

She's not sure, she's been out of town. She assures me that there's some fancy scientific goop inside that's keeping everything in order and of course I asked...

'How do you know? Do you ever take Tui out, ya know, and pet him? Take him for a walk?'

'Tui's a girl and of course I don't take her for a walk,' she claims.

I say, 'well what's the point of keeping her if you're not gonna at least play with her and snuggle or something?'

She shows me to the door and promises to come get Tui in the morning. Here I am, standing in the hallway with a room temperature Cockatoo that's been dead for five years. What just happened?

The next morning she came and got him at 8:30, which really pissed me off. I was thinking 10 or 11. She didn't sleep well at all. Too worried about Tui. I didn't sleep either, I just laid there listening to that refrigerator hum and every time that icemaker dropped a load I thought Tui was springing back to life and trying to get out. Flappin around in my freezer.

What the hell is in that canister!? What if I opened it up and something really scary sprung out at me like a dusty old lady ghost or an alien gooey flying lizard fired right out of one of those fake cans of nuts and it tried to bite me and chased me all over my new babe lair? What if it got some of that nasty slimy slobbery stuff all over my new couch?

That's what I did all nite long, just freaked

myself right out. And of course she was not the least bit appreciative or thankful in the morning. They never are. Like I just held the door for her or watered a plant or something.

Psycho.

I cannot believe I didn't open that stupid thing and look inside. I've got to know. She owes me.

I'm going down there tomorrow and...

I'll let ya know.

RV

2001

My parents, Bud and Carolyn have a recreational vehicle. An RV. They used to have one of those huge, really long ones that go about 40 MPH, get 3 MPG and seem to only fit in the fast lane. Lots of bumper stickers. Their tastes have evolved over the years and now they're sportin a souped-up Van, with strategically arranged beds, baby fridge, microwave and showerito. Very efficient.

They get restless there in Paris, and join up with several other retired friends from all over, and they just take off. Branson, was of course the hot spot for years, but now it's much too touristy. Dollywood? You betcha.

The Rockies, Grand Canyon, Florida, and every flea market in between.

They have walkie-talkies, but all they ever seem to say, is... "Shorty, You back there? Over. There's a Cracker Barrel up ahead, over. Watch out for that Possum, over." They follow me around sometimes.

I'm singing an opera in Seattle, or Salt Lake City, or Santa Fe, and in rolls a squadron of RVs. They play dress up and come to the opera, and I swear one night, during *Madama Butterfly*, I could hear Bud snorin out there. We cook on the grill and sit outside and take walks and we play dominos and 42 and cards and we laugh. We laugh a lot more than you would imagine. No TV, no movies, we just entertain each other.

They'd rather sleep in that thing than the finest bed at the Waldorf. I'm like, Mom, I have a huge house here, this kitchen is gorg! Come on in! But she's in that RV rockin chair, hummin spirituals and reading her daily bible lesson and shuckin corn and shellin peas and snappin beans and slicin up fresh maters from the garden.

Two years ago I was in San Francisco, performing in the World Premiere production of Andre Previns' *A Streetcar Named Desire*. Kind of a big deal. I got an under the table permission slip and Bud hooked up the RV in the parking lot of the opera house. After the Sunday Matinee we returned to find that the fella who took their $10 parking fee, in the free lot, was most likely the one who broke the windows and helped himself to Bud and Carolyns' stuff. Nothing is Sacred.

We're sitting around waiting for the police to arrive, and Lotfi Mansouri walks by. He runs the San Francisco Opera. He's the gentleman who hired me, and he's also an important director. I make introductions all the way around, I'm squirmin and fidgety because I'm not quite sure how Lotfi feels about five big RV's plugged up behind the War Memorial Opera House.

But next thing ya know, we're sitting in the lawn chairs, drinking iced tea, Reba and Shorty and Bob and Viola bring BBQ Brisket and cheesy potatoes and blackberry cobbler with Blue Bell Ice Cream. They give Lotfi the RV tour, proudly pointing out the features. They looked at engines and talked about retirement and travel and Texas, and favorite places and gas mileage and towing capacity. And we played ourselves a very competitive little Domino tournament.

Lotfi impressed the hell out of me that day. He sat with us common folk and played games and listened to our stories and our songs and looked at pictures of the grandchildren, and he laughed a lot. I think he enjoyed the RV.

Now, I know he retired this year, and I wonder...

GUNTA

2002

I have spent my first two weeks here in Frankfurt, Germany, feeling good and sorry for myself. You've heard it before, stranger in a foreign land, lonely, doesn't speak the language, feeling all outcast and scorned. Self-pity can be remarkably therapeutic, I seem to enjoy it. Shut up, this is hard sometimes. I'm in the cab coming into the city and my driver chuckles... 'A Texan zinging Wagner in Germany? Oh zay going love you!'

This from a man named Helmut Knobler.

I packed for summer and it is cold and it has rained 10 days straight and I'm chilly and soggy all the time and it makes me cranky. I can't find my way around, don't know a soul, nicht sprechen sie Deutsch sehr guten, but mostly it's the little things I miss like TV, like movies in Englisch, like Dominoes pizza and KFC. Like a decent hot shower!

And then I sit there at rehearsal and they're all engaged in some heated, deep discussion about production values or music or motivation and everyone's excited or argumentative and opinionated and then they turn to the class clown over here and say, 'Stand over there, sing pretty.' I'm picking up more and more of it, but I'm not tellin.

Alas and alack, I am proud to report the tide has turned. Jetlag and a little infection, gone at last. A few days ago I got up early, feeling kinda perky and decided to take myself a little walk, see some other areas of town. Woopty doop, the sun is even threatening to come out. Not two blocks from where I live I found the most gorgeous park. Who knew? Gigantic, ancient trees, lush green meadows and fountains and sculptures and birds a-singin and children frolickin and laughin and playin and music and pooches and picnickin and drinkin and smoochin. Just what I needed.

So I've begun a ritual, a morning walk in the

park. It's probably about 5 square miles round the whole thing, I'm guessing. Good for the body and the soul.

Over in the far back corner, I spy a little gate, shrubs and flowers and trees hiding what's behind. I'm going for a look. It's a garden. Ein garten. It's HUGE and it is lovely. And it seems to be measured off into individual little plots. Lots of folks back here working, mostly seniors, but a few young people. There are stone sheds creating a border of sorts, where they keep all their tools and such. No locks. I learn that you can lease out one of these plots and do with it as you wish.

I'm wandering around, taking in the flowers and fruit and veggies and such, some of these things I've never seen before, and I made a friend. Her back was stiff from hoeing, and she was stretching out over by the fence. Her name is Gunta. Funny name if you ask me. Gunta is zweiundsiebzig jahre. 72. She speaks about as much Englisch as I do Deutsch, so we're kinda helpin each other out. Teaching each other a little bit. I say flower, she says Blume. I say tree, she says Baum.

She's got two of these gardens, right next to

each other, one for her and one for her late husband Christof, who passed away last year. They worked together here at this same spot for 50 (funfzig) years. Can you imagine? She sings while she works. I told her I'm gezingin at the Opern and she insists I should leave the zingin to her. She thinks I'll scare the blumen and she's probably right. We got your carroten und tomaten und turnips und strawberries over hier, jasmine and honeysuckle along the fence. Christof loved the flowers so we got all kinds growing on his side.

It's an awful lot of work for her to do by herself so she asks me if... 'Mochten Sie, mich hilfen?'

'Ja, I would love to help.'

So, things are looking up. We meet three mornings a week. I'm going to do a little zingin, a little farmin, a little blumen.

Me and Gunta.

Und no more whining.

SCALDED DOG

2004

Tonight I feel like I made my first appearance on the Jerry Springer Show. Just a supporting character, I pray. No headline tomorrow, no local news, no horrible statistic, no Court TV exclusive, I pray.

It was just two nights ago that I sang at a fundraiser for the Metropolitan Opera in NYC. They rented out a Broadway theater and we presented the play "Master Class", with eight different leading ladies playing the role of Maria Callas. They each did a scene and you'll never believe it, but I did mine with Kathy Bates. Yes I did. And then we all went out to dinner and I sat right there between

Kathy and Jessica. Jessica Lange! I giggled and stared like an idiot the whole time, just couldn't help myself.

And now, having been essentially homeless for these past three years, I return to the family fold back in Texas. I'm just mindin my own business, eating dinner at my Momma's table and my sistern Kelli says, 'Jay, you should give Lindsay a call, she's so cute!'

And I'm like, 'Well, yeah, but she's got an eight month old baby girl and a four year old son.'

And Kelli says, 'Well, yeah, but she's divorced now.'

'Well, so? Only for two months.'

'But it's been bad for a really long time. Her husband is a crazy hillbilly.'

But you know what, I like Lindsay, we were friends in college, and why shouldn't I call an old friend and play a little catch-up? Right? I'm not home very often. What's the harm, right? So I call her and she says 'come on out about 10, the baby be sleepin by then.' They live in the Boondocks in a little cluster with all their Kinfolk. I arrive at the appointed hour and we sit and sip Boone's Farm Strawberry Wine and we're chattin away and laughing and telling stories and remembering and reminiscing and ya know what? This is actually a lot of fun. And I start to relax a little when there's a knock on the door. It's almost midnight.

I know right away, there's evil out there on that stoop. The hair on the back of my... well, the hair on my back stood up, came a-bristlin right out of my shirt and the coyotes were howlin and the clouds covered the moon and I felt the chill in the air that can only spell Angry Redneck. Seems the four-year old son, who I was never formally introduced to, wanted to sleep with his Momma. Fair enough. Divorced Dad Billy Bob brings him over. He seemed none too impressed with my Mom's Buick out front cuz he came a stormin into the house wantin to know just what the bleepity bleep is goin on in here!? He's none too pleased to meet me.

He's a pretty big fella, bigger than me, he is country fried and he's got a full-on Mullet and a long Goatee accessorized with what appears to be mac and cheese. Of course he's got on boots and a dirty wife beater. The boy is screamin and cryin and Lindsay is hollerin at Bubba and tellin me to just sit down I ain't goin nowhere... and I say I think maybe I oughta mosey along about now... and Jethro yells, 'Nu-Uh! Nu-Uh!' as he looks at the wine jug. 'No yer not drinking wine in my house with my wife and baby, damn right you better git outta here M....r F.....r SumB..tch.' And the obscenities that spewed forth along with quite a remarkable amount of spittle and elbow macaroni, and the screaming of children and Tammy Wynette on the radio... well, it was just too much for me. I started laughin. I really shouldn't have, but I couldn't help it. A sputtering giggle at first, but that just made him mad, and as I made my surprisingly nimble escape, Leroy started chasin me off the porch and around the yard. Two grown men running around in the dark.

And I can't stop laughin and he is clearly going to whoop my ass if he ever catches me. We pause on opposite sides of his truck, lookin at each other thru the dirty windows, winded, he's cussin, she's screamin, the babies are all crying, I'm beggin him... 'I'm sooooowrry, just let me go hoooome... I'll never come back agiiiiiin, let me git on my horse and ride on out of tooown!'

But here he comes chasin again... It was so funny. It was so frightening. So absolutely surreal, because ya never know just how something like this might end. He finally realized he'll never catch me, as I am quite fleet of foot... no, he needs his gun. So there he goes, roarin off, sprayin us all down with dirt and pebbles. Now was that necessary?

I was out of there quicker than a scalded dog, headed the other direction. And now as I sit here sleepless in my Momma's house, I've gotta wonder... is that John Boy I see out there in his Truck right now? Got a dip of snuff and he's spitting in a beer bottle listening to George Jones, expertly balancing his Deer rifle with night vision, lining me up twixt the crosshairs?

Sure hope that's the end of it.

That's Kathy Bates. Told ya so.

FLAG FOOTBALL

2004

I'm not sure just when, but at some point here recently I became a spectator. More reading and ordering-in and watching TV and less and less time out participating in the real world. I'm very upset! It's not that I'm a big ole sissy, really it's not, but we are most often alone out here on the operatic trail. Tho for a while I admit this artsy, glamorous, world traveler, hotel, room service kinda lifestyle was very well suited to my LazyBoy personality, it has now lost much of its appeal.

I think it turned sour here, since it's February in Toronto. It's freezing cold and snows or sleets all day long and I just don't wanna go out in that mess. So spank me.

But I do love to watch. I have this gorgeous view over the city, but it's the playground right across the street that has really held my attention for these seven weeks. I love the sound of those kids out frolicking at recess, they wake me up every morning. That's even better than a thunderstorm, or the ocean. I guess cause none of them kids are mine.

I watch them faithfully with my morning coffee and I am utterly amazed at how much screaming and laughing and crying these children squeeze into one hour. We got your soccer, two or three games of whiffle ball, your jumping of ropes, swinging from bars, Hopping of Scotch, tag, and of course, the all-time fav, dodge ball. Whose dumb idea was this game? Here, let's pound each other in the head with rubber balls. And no mercy on those sissy girls! I've got my eye on that big kid and I swear if he pulls her hair one more time I'm gonna...

There's a running track around this big grass field, well I think there's grass under all that snow and mud, and ya know what? Not one of those kids is out there running around that track. Ya know why? Cause it's just not fun. These kids are all about the pursuit of fun. That's what I'm missing, see? Where's the fun? So anyway, it's Saturday, and for this time and place my perfectly dreary afternoon looks pretty good. I spy some grownups out there and they're playing good ole American football. Sorta. It started out as flag football, and quickly turned into organized mud wrestling. They're young adults, mid-twenties, two girls on each team, whoopin it up, all lookin happy and healthy out there, coulda been a Wheaties or a J Crew commercial. I wanted to smack em all, out there carryin on like that havin all that fun!

And then it happened. The Alpha Male spotted me way up here on my perch, ever on the balcony, and as if pinched on the behind by the strong hand of fate, he calls out 'Come on down, we need one more.' Just terrific. I pretend not to hear, and then that, that, cute perky bubbly blondy girly said, 'Come out and play, if your Mommy says it's OK...'

Now what do I do? I'm thinking... I'm a grown Man, and it's muddy out there, I'll ruin some perfectly clean clothes, I, I, I'm too tired, I will surely get hurt, yeah, that's it...

someone might kick me in the, in the throat, and I'll lose my delicate voice, and it's misting out there and I might catch cold.

WHAT IS WRONG WITH ME?!

I am the Biggest Wuss to ever own a Chevy truck. It's a game of flag frickin football! And I am not too old, or too fat, or too lazy, and Gosh Darnet, I will Bitchslap the sleeping demon of my idleness and go out there and have me some fun!

And I did. Sucked in my gut and held my breath as I bounded onto that mud soaked field. Up close, I'm pleased to be twice the size of Mr. Alpha Male, and I'm kinda liking my chances here on the field of play.

We huddle up and I look blondy in the eye and thru gritted teeth, I say, 'Just get me the ball.' I did indeed get that filthy slimy ball, and I tucked it away somewhere outta sight and started the train and I'm tellin ya, I ran smack over every one of them, boys and girls alike, some of em twice, I'm swatting them away like flies and I scored myself the finest touchdown of my life!

Oh, The Glory! My Youth, My Vigor! My teammates marvel, they cheer, they praise and they dog pile. All on top of Me, their Hero! We wallow in the mud, and for that one precious moment, I was truly madly deeply happy. All was right with the world.

Tho a videotape for posterity woulda been nice. On the second play of my Canadian Football career, I'm galopping down the field, warp speed for me, and I slipped. Nary a soul within ten yards of me. My right foot went forward and my left foot stayed backward and with tongue floppin out, I touched my right knee with my chin for the first time in 20 years.

Fun is over. Two plays. Nine stitches it took, to piece my tongue and bottom lip back together.

Oh, the shame. Blondy went with me to the Emergency Room, but it was too much to bear and I screamed at her, 'Just Go! Don't look at me! I'm Hideous!'

I have a show tomorrow night. Thank God, it's in Russian, maybe no one will notice.

STEPS

2008

At 6 AM on that Saturday Spring morning, me and my best friends in the whole wide world boarded the long retired Bluebird School Bus, now owned and operated by the good Brethren of The Immanuel Baptist Church. And we made haste for Six Flags over Texas! I was but 14 years old and giddy as a wee little girl. I'd heard legends and tales of terrifying roller coasters and log rides down white water rapids and loopty loops and the food and the people and the buckets of joy and delight that can be consumed all in one day.

My first time and Oh! How we lived!

And on that very same nite, a concert was presented in what they called The Amphitheater. Larry Gatlin and the Gatlin Brothers Band. Traditional good ole boy country gospel four part harmonies and guitars and lights and drums and fiddles and mandolins and electronic keyboards. Markus Hardy on my left, John David and Patrick on my right. Of course I'd never seen anything like it. Never heard men sing together like that. Larry told stories and sang songs that he wrote himself and he played the coolest guitar I'd ever seen. It's called an Ovation. The back of this beatific acoustic guitar did not look like wood, but rather some synthetic man-made poly-carbon Star Trek stuff, and how he made it sing.

My innocent young mind was soundly blown that nite. I knew before the first song was over what I wanted to do with my life, who I wanted to be. I will be Larry Gatlin and I will play that fab guitar and I will tell stories and people will laugh. I will write and sing and entertain all the days of my life.

Of course I didn't know how to play the guitar, so I went and got myself a job at the Fuller Furniture Store right off the square in lovely downtown Paris. I vacuumed and dusted and delivered and polished and cleaned the bathrooms and the kitchen after school and on Saturdays and I saved my money until at last, my Momma drove me all the way to Fort Worth, where I did purchase a replica of that very same Ovation guitar. Then I took some lessons and learned to play it a little.

At age 16, I got my big break in show business: I was asked to sing at The Great First Baptist Church on a blessed Sunday nite! They broadcast the service Live on the Radio! All my friends can listen in! And here's the thing, I wasn't even a member at that church! It was like a real, professional engagement.

This, was, the, big time.

Of course I chose to play my swanky new guitar and sing one of Larry's best gospel songs.

And it went just fine. Not great, but fine. I sat on a stool with my right foot up on a crossbar, guitar resting on my thigh, and before I even started playing or singing, that foot started bobbing up and down with great agitation. I was a bit nervy. I could not make it stop. And so I admittedly did not play my best or sing my best because my whole body was shimmyin, shakin, and perceptibly quakin.

Not conducive.

But ya know what, the audience clapped anyway, like I was Larry Gatlin himself. Some of those old Deacons called out 'Amen! Amen'! Which I think means, 'You were awesome!' And right there on the second row, my first ever girlfriend Kristi Young sat beaming up at me. Like I was Elvis.

My heart did swell, my chest did poof, and as I waved my love back to the adoring fans, I missed that first step. And I fell. Face forward, head down, limbs splayed prostrate, and I bounced on my chin all the way down to the auditorium floor. Rug burn. Disgrace.

The Pastor voiced faux concern laced with a giggle, and soon everyone joined in with a hearty harr harr. They laughed out loud and pointed at my shame. Not very Christian, but luckily, I'm tough.

The best part is that the name of the song was, 'Steps'.

True story.

Thirty years later I entered the stage door at the Cobb Energy Center, in Atlanta, Georgia. It was our opening nite and I was to sing Erik in Wagner's *Der Fliegende Holländer*. The Flying Dutchman. And there in the hallway stood Larry Gatlin. I have not seen him in person since that fateful nite at Six Flags.

So I gushed. I stammered. I wept a little as I told him my story, how I loved that concert and his music and command and charisma, how I wanted to be just like him. He was in turn more than a little curious about how a concert he sang in 1978 led me to be an opera zinger. Whole other story, I assured.

And then the benevolent Hand of Fate intervened. It turns out that Larry's very good friend is a member of the Atlanta Opera Board of Directors, and they arranged a fundraiser, an evening with sorta thing…. and Mark Delavan (The Dutchman) and I, played and sang with Larry Gatlin. I sang "Steps" for the first time in 20 years.

Now, I've had some good nites. I've performed on some fine stages. But on this night, the circle that is my life feels complete.

And oh so sweet.

SIDE OF FRIES

2007

You'd never believe it, but there are everyday ordinary good folks out there who will fly across the world to see an opera. Then turn around and go right back home. It's true.

Maybe it's to see Wagner's *Ring*, lots of big fans out there for that one. Maybe it's to hear a certain soprano or a young baritone who is just all the rage. Some favor the string quartet. Sometimes they sponsor a young conductor or director and help them get their career started or pay for their schooling or some such. Some folks just love music so much they don't mind flying all that way one bit, just to hear it live, sitting right out there in that auditorium.

It's true.

I gotta tell ya, my very favorite part of the whole showbiz operatic affair is when the orchestra tunes, and they usually do it at least twice. I love that sound, because once they get started each player can just do whatever he wants, a scale or a melody or that one passage he always screws up or perhaps one big loud note over and over, and it is just a noisy chaotic mess. That sound means you better straighten up and get ready! Then that one person with the most expensive violin stands up and says, 'all right, simmer down, simmer down.'

So they do.

Every orchestra in the world has that one fella who every single time has to play the last bit all by himself.

Nobody likes that guy.

The Thompsons from San Francisco... they come to hear me sing every now and then; they have for ten years. I couldn't believe it at first, was sure there was some mistake, but they will get on an airplane and fly somewhere they don't live just to see me in an opera. Even my own Momma will tell ya that's kinda crazy. I never know whenst nor wherst they're coming, they just show up there at my dressing room every once in a while, smiling and proud as can be. Mostly here in the US, but last year in Amsterdam, there they were after an uplifting performance of *Doctor Atomic.*

Harold and Gilly grew up in England, but took a fancy to our West Coast years ago. They raised their children here, taught literature and geology at one of our finest.

Last night at our opening of *Fidelio,* someone had the poor manners to barf right outside the very stage door of our theatre.

Not friendly.

Hopefully that was not a commentary on our efforts. I don't know exactly when said yarkage appeared, but it was still steamy when I walked out.

So I reckon what's happened is the guard back here was notified, and so he or some other in authority deigned to construct a most flimsy rudimentary elastic barrier of sorts. If you will, liken it to those guiding us to and through the slaughterhouse or the refreshment counter or airport security. And whilst trying to keep all the lovely, fancy, wealthy audience members on their way home bedect in Evening Formal Wear and jewels and luxury automobiles… while trying to discourage them from waltzing right thru it, we actors, players, craftsmen are led straight into the very mouth of it, indeed. No guard on hand to say, 'be mindful, watch your step, there is a rather large pool of vomitus a mere five paces outside this very door.'

Nope, nary a warning.

Luckily, I did witness the bassoonist slide in her heels, turn her ankle, then drag her black dress right thru the heart of it not three feet in front of me.

Terribly unfortunate. He he.

And not the least bit funny. He he.

At this most awkward and shocking juncture, Harold and Gilly appear on the other side of the tether and clasp me to their collective bosoms. Bosoms'es?

'Well look who's heah,' I exclaim in my finest Posh British accent. We exchange surprised pleasantries and salutations and how mahvelous, and oh the production values and how gorgeous to see you, the second act trio was divine, and oh look, it's the Maestro, we heard him last year in Worcestershire, and but of course he'd love to sign your program, Maestro do come hither…

See, once they get all fired up it's hard to slow the train.

They loves them some opera.

I'm trying to pay attention, but some dank curiosity compels me to have a little looky over at… ieuw… looks like orange soda, and… curly fries.

Yes, it is.

Oh, urrp.

That's nasty.

The back of my throat feels squiggly and I

think I can smell it.

For some reason, it reminds me of last year when Meg and I were in Tokyo, in this really swank International Hotel named after Prince Takanohana, whom I believe is a Sumo Wrestler. One night I had an orange soda from the mini-bar and called down to room service for a Bucket of Ice. A Bucket of Ice.

These people speak way better English than we do Japanese, I'll tell ya that right off... but, still.

The eager fella replied... 'Uh, you wan bag o lice?'

'No thank you, just a bucket of ice.'

'Uh, Brucket of mice?'

'Ice, not mice.'

'Uh, you wan Pad of Rice? Bracket o pies? Sac o flies? Lucky stwikes? Side of Fries?'

'Yes prease.'

And we just laughed ourselves blue. Seriously.

I had to go find a Japanese Pharmacy in the middle of the nite and get a totally foreign Bronchiole Inhaler, cuz Meg laughed herself directly into the throes a bona fide asthma attack.

I didn't even know she had asthma.

And just how do I manage to communicate with these worldly folks you might wonder? It's all in the hand signals and facial gesticulations.

I'll show ya sometime.

See, ya can't just keep sayin the same thing over and over, louder and slower, like... 'She cain't breeeathe... She cain't breeeathe.'

They just don't understand good English like mine.

Anyway, I got the puffer and Meg survived. But now, sometimes she kinda holds back even when I'm being super funny, cuz she says she's scairt she'll laugh too hard and I'll have to run out to the Walgreens.

That suddenly reeks of insincerity.

Where was I? So, by now back at our opening nite, there are volunteers on hand to kindly spread the word... 'oooh, be careful, don't step in that, watch out, no no don't look, here take my hand, come this way.'

One old duder said, 'Would ya look at these Animals, they don't even bother to chew their food anymore, there are two whole Curly fries right there... Damn kids these days.'

I'm smiling and looking Gilly right in the face when another passerby points out... 'That's Orangina, I threw that up in the 9th grade at a soccer game. Haven't touched it since.'

His hippie girlfriend says, 'Tomorrow, you should just drink one, or like, an Orange Julius ya know, just get over it.'

Jonathon, tenor, lovely chap, rollerblading his way out the door didst not slow down to greet me or my friends, who unawares of the atrocities nearby have carried on with much enthusiasm for some five minutes now about I don't know what... I haven't heard a word. I'm just noddin and trying not to spit up in my mouth. Jonathon spins off and his left skate hits the puddle and skids on a curly fry, but he rights the ship in the nic.

'Ieuw, what was that?'

'Nothing at all, carry on.

Well done, you.'

So anyway, I guess what I'm trying to say, if I'm pressed to make a point here, is... You better watch out, you better pay attention, it doesn't matter how pretty you are or how clever you are or how much money you've got, if you are not careful you will step right in the big fat middle of somebody else's nasty mess.

And we will all laugh at you.

For once in my life, I didn't.

HUMBLE PIE

2004

Well, I've been served yet another generous slice of humble pie. A shameful indignity dealt by the cruel hand of fate. Or maybe it was just bad timing.

My Mom had shoulder replacement surgery last Monday, and for once in my life I get to be home to maybe do a little good, help out a bit.

Don't get me wrong, more than anything else I have bickered with everyone in town over absolutely nothing. Bud says I change the channel too fast. Do Not. He dishes his crafty vengeance in the form of Gene Autrey Western Musical Marathons.

I cannot grasp the fact that my brother-in-law did all that work on the old Ford truck, then painted it the gaudiest, ugliest dull shineless color d'orange that the good folks at Home Depot can whip up. What was he thinking? My best friend Mark will not accept the fact that Pavarotti is a better singer than Merle Haggard.

This very morning at breakfast my Mom spread the joyful news that she discovered three tea stains that must be shampooed out of the Buick's beige carpet. I'm driving the Buick, clearly my doing. Tea. Beige. I'm not seeing the problem. She then presented me with a no-spill tumbler from the super size Wal-Mart that looks more like a glorified sippy cup for some clumsy toddler. Told me to show a little respect.

I decided I'd just borrow a bicycle from Jeff and kill two birds with one cow-patty... get my lazy behind some cardio exercise and escape the fear of ever spilling another beverage in the Buick. I got about halfway across town on that rusty old bike and had to beg Bud to come fetch me in his pickup truck. Hush, it was hot and humid and that little bitty seat makes me very nervous.

Anyway, my one week home has turned into five, and so I busy myself about the house, helping Mom with her physical therapy and doing the laundry and dishes and weeding the flowerbed and feeding the critters and such. I am also becoming quite the entrepreneur, out there grooming little old ladies yards for $15 a pop, then of course paying my nephew Hunter $5 to actually perform the uh, what do you call it? The manual labor.

Suckers.

Anyway, it's dinnertime and I smell like the tool shed so I jump in the shower. My sistern Kelli is on her way over to take some of this food away before I eat myself into some Serious Southern Fried acid reflux. As I exit the shower I just assumed that was Kelli's voice I was hearing out in the living room. I'm all wet and hairy and lotioned up, with a twenty-year-old shriveled crusty white towel straining against my ample waist. I had to fetch the pad lock from my gym bag to hold it somewhat sorta semi shut.

Just before I step into the living room, let's just agree that I made a rather boisterous comment on Ms. Betty's Mexican three bean casserole that I enjoyed for lunch.

Not pretty, not gentlemanly, but kinda funny, and I was laughing out loud, scrubbin my ear with a Q-tip as I round the corner and came face to face with Mrs. Josephine Gambill. Oh. Hi, Mrs. Fortenbury. Mrs. Reba. Five lovely little ladies from my Mother's Bible study group. They're having Iced Tea and Bundt cake and praying for Carolyn and I'm wearing a grin and a wetnap. What can I do now? They've seen me.

As I try to make my escape Miss Reba voices concern over my situation, ya know, being 40 and homeless and loveless, jobless, penniless, living with my parents. She fears I might be depressed and proudly reports that Crockett Middle School needs a choir teacher. I should go apply; she thinks they'd be happy to have me. Swaim's Hardware is hiring and so is Campbell Soup, but only the night shift.

They take turns dispensing golden nuggets of wisdom; a bird in hand is worth three in the bush and so forth. I can't tell if they are really concerned for my plight or just poking fun.

I assure them that I feel quite liberated from

all those material things that tie a person down and I am very confident that I will be paid to sing opera again one day. Half-naked as I am, I go ahead and boldly sing… "Life, is just a bowl, of cherries, don't take it serious, life's too mysterious…"

They are not convinced.

Monita and JoAnne insist that I come sit down so they can pray for me, and tho I am humiliated and sweating profusely, I sit amongst them and start praying for me too.

I'm beginning to think maybe I need it.

WINSTON AND JIM

2005

Ya know, I meet some very interesting people in this line of work. I've learned to expect the worst, and I am rarely disappointed. Folks like you and me, who just spend too much time alone, maybe in the practice room, in front of the mirror, watching their every twitch, admiring every nuance of their lovely voice. Too much time alone in hotel rooms, eating out, reading, studying, exercising... always alone. No wonder so many of us think the world revolves around us, our little world does.

We make lots of fluffy faux friendships, cordial little encounters with colleagues we don't really like. But hey, we never have time to nurture anything more meaningful, more lasting. We won't see em again for a year, if then, and then we will talk about the same things --- technique, managers, who got this job I shoulda got, politics of opera, dreadfully boring.

Well, I've met a couple of fellas here recently that are very unique, indeed. Let me tell you about Jim. He's a cowboy of some sort, methinks. He wears the hat, the boots, his hands are like rawhide, he's got a big beard and a shiny western belt. His shirt buttons are pearl and they snap. First time I saw him, he was playing with a Barbie doll... I walked over to him and said, in my finest 5 year old lilt... 'Well who is this ya got here? She's a pretty little thang, can I hold her?'

All right I didn't say it, but I thought it.

See, Big Jim does make-up for the opera. He puts on my makeup. He also does amazing work on dolls. Restores them, re-wigs them, makes clothes for them. In truth, he is a craftsman. He sews, he rebuilds cars. He paints. He whittles. Now who do ya know anymore that whittles? Nobody whittles. He makes things patiently, with great care, with his own two hands, and then he gives them away. Been working on Christmas gifts for his grandchildren for six months. I'm lucky if I can spend twenty minutes in some sorry mall pickin out some chintzy little piece of nothing for people that I really do care about. Maybe it's time to change my ways.

He speaks softly and eloquently. He's making a Vestment right now for a friend who is going into the Priesthood, and you should see this thing. Beautiful, a work of art. I love this man, he is so many things I want to be some day, when I grow up.

And let me tell you about Winston. I've seen him around the Opera House here for the past four years, but never worked with him till this show. This one's about St. Francis of Assisi and I get to wear a fat suit. Super fun.

The first time I met Winston, he got a tear in his eye, and he told me he had just lost someone named Jay. His partner for 47 years. Calls him My Jay, when we talk. Winston is tiny. Maybe 5'4", 130 lbs. Always wears his Sunday best, and these snazzy little glasses. He set em down on the counter the other day and when he was out I tried them on. 'Most fetching,' I said out loud, then saw him standing in the door. Busted. He wants me to have them. No really... I think he's gonna give me his glasses, just because I liked them.

He's probably 75 years old. He's a dresser. Know what that is? I'm a little ashamed to say... he organizes my costumes, lays them out, helps me squiggle into that fat suit, tucks in my shirt tail, he'll tie my shoes if I let him! Little old man doing every little thing for me. He brings me grapes on show days, washes em just right. He says they'll give me energy. Ya know what he says before I go out on stage? 'Give em Heaven.'

It always gives me pause. He really wants me to be great.

When I come off the stage he is right there with a hanky and a bottle of water, and with a smile he says, 'Ya done good kiddo,' even when I don't.

I developed an immediate fondness for little Winston. I made suppositions and assumptions, not really judgments... just, ya know, how we take in people when we first meet. I saw who he was and what he does and

I like him.

Then I found out he served in WW 2. On a submarine. He was a Sonar and Radar specialist. Twenty years old and he caught tuberculosis down there in that sub in the Pacific Ocean. He spent a total of three years in a Veterans hospital, much of that time with one lung deflated intentionally. Can you imagine the misery he must have witnessed? Can you imagine laying in a hospital bed waiting to die for three years? He couldn't breathe.

Later, he went to Columbia University, became a writer, a college professor, poetry and arts and such... and now he works at the Opera House, just because he loves it. This sweet little old man holding out my pants.

How nice, how rare, these two gentlemen who do what they want, what they enjoy, what gives them joy. I feel honored to know them.

I hope you liked them.

LA MOUCHE

2008

Here I am in Paris, France, the most romantic city in the world, a Newlywed without his Bride. I know better than to bellyache, but Meg is the best travel companion a fella could hope for and I surely do miss her. She'll be here next Tuesday and what fun we shall have!

I'm singing a small role in the world premiere of *The Fly*, here at the historic Théâtre du Châtelet.

"La Mouche", as they call it round here. It is based on the movie and will be directed and written by film legends David Cronenberg and Howard Shore, conducted by Plácido

Domingo.

Should be super cool, don't ya think? I play a drunk redneck in a bar who gets his arm snapped in two by that fella who's turning into a fly. Come on, admit it, I've got a groovy job.

Now I confess I've been downright lazy my first few weeks over here; I reckon because so little is required of me. I only sing for about five minutes. Being here in this city all alone has given me time aplenty for reflection and circumspection. Why just yesterday I waxed myself nostalgic, remembering times past, how truly broke I was, how I did fret and moan and pace the floor, and practice and study and dream of travel and adventure and artistic fulfillment and abundance and how I waited not so patiently for that call to come, just one morsel of favorable news that someone would indeed pay me to sing.

How I did take up vows and oaths that if I might get just that one truly Plum job I shall be most grateful and would ne'er besmirch the Fates and the Gods on High again. Well behold, they have delivered a Plum. Many, in fact. And I do hereby renew my vow to be thankful evermore, for certainly we know not when, if ever, we shall taste these Plums again.

Anyway, hippie, I nodded off last nite reading "The Poisonwood Bible", which by the by is not at all what it sounds like. I awoke at 8, much too early for a rainy day stuffed poppin full of nothing to do, so I dozed back in, that deep, dreamy, twitchy, drooly, hibernative sleep... I'm just kiddin, I don't drool... until the cleaning lady came in and woke me right up.

I'm sprawled on my side, facing away from the bedroom door, the sheets a useless heap upon the floor, just nekid as I can be.

Clutching my favorite super soft pillow that travels the world with me. She just came right on in and started squealing in French, this maid who I now know comes on Thursday.

Ya see, the doorbell here is a chirping bird. The bird didst chirp several times I do vaguely recall, but who would think a chirping bird requires any response on my part at all? I had my earplugs in, my eye mask on, and I didn't know she was even in the building till she started hollerin not three feet away. She's retrieving the clean linens she just sent flying, I'm scrambling, sitting up halfway to a heart attack wondering where on earth I am and what's going on and wasting way too much time extricating the earplugs and removing said eye mask without proper attention and expedition given to the covering of the heiney and the doodle. Both of us just screaming.

I've heard tell that these Europeans are super evolved and comfortable with their nudity. Trust me, she weren't with mine. It was 11:45am and she had no reason to expect there would be a nekid, hairy man still in bed. That'll learn her. She's crying and I'm pretty sure I'll be making an appearance in her nightmares ce soir, n'est ce pas? Maybe her therapy sessions too.

There is of course no moral to the story, but it gave me pause... has the time come that I must sleep in pajamas, buttons and all? Am I of that age when there's a good chance that someone I don't know or I've forgotten all about will just waltz right on in, further demoralizing and degrading my dwindling dilapidated dignity? No, I declare, I shall indeed sleep as nekid and as deeply as I please.

Consider yourself warned.

And try knocking next time.

WUBY THUE

2008

It's been two days since we got back home from Paris, France, and we're in the Walgreens Pharmacy at seven in the morning, dazed and confused cuz we're still on that European inner time clock. Meg is over in the drop-off line and I'm wandering around perusing the latest holiday sweetie offerings and daydreaming and sorta woozy with the jet-lag and the gentleman with the intercom says…'Ugh, Meesa, uh, Yay Mauweeth, Meesa uh, Yay Mauweeth, prease to frun, prease to frun.'

I admire the Bag of Halloween Reese's King Size Pumpkin Butter Cups and ponder to myself, did he just call my name? Surely not.

Then I went and got some milk.

Few minutes later, he said it again.

Yay Mauweeth.

Is that me? Am I indeed, Yay Mauweeth?

I giggled and decided, well I sure am.

Went up front and told him so.

After flexing my mad skills with transliterations, I gleaned that my rife Peg was in brack, she no free gooo.

'You got the wrong fella,' I inform. 'That's my rife over there in the…'

Rah roh.

I went out brack to the loading dock and there she is with the Frito Lay woman standing there looking down at her all sprawled out on the concrete pavement just sweatin in her prettiest white summer dress.

She no free gooo. Almost made it to the toilette when she took a knee.

Frito Pie says, 'she just fell over, I din't touch her.'

'Ok. Thanks. Preciate cha. Nice Pants.'

Calm reassurances and mopping of brows and Gatorade and saltines follow. Since we're in the Walgreens anyway, I put her in a Rascal and rode her over to the blood pressure machine where sure nuf, hers is way too low and she's looking rather peekid and ye ole Apothecary behind yon counter proclaims that I better take her to the Emergency Room or something dramatic like that tout suite.

'You just simmer down', says I, 'and while you're at it why don't ya run get us one of them EPT tests.'

Just in case.

So he did, and I made the executive diskizion that maybe what she really needs is a proper Whopper with cheese from the Burger King. That makes me feel a whole lot better than sitting around with a bunch of nasty sick people at the Doc in the Box or the E.R.

But this isn't about me, it's about Meg and it

turns out the King did not make her free gooo.

Sawwy.

What seems like just a few minutes ago… we dreamed a little dream that we would get ourselves good and pregnant while we were over there in Paris, this summer. Super Romantic.

And… I did it!

I mean, we did it.

We's gonna have us a baby!

Can't tell ya why, but we have felt in our souls that she's a wittle girl. Looks like her Momma, I'm sure hoping. And as I envision my future and that one most super fun moment of them all… my baby can just barely walk and talk and when I ask what her name is… she smiles and says, 'Wuby Thue.'

Because her cheeks are so chubby!

Go on, say it out loud one time, Wuby Thue. What a day of rejoicing that will be.

Ruby Sue, that's what we've been calling her for these past six months.

Now ya look up and we are extremely pregnant and equally unprepared.

Meg has been truly stellar. Exemplary. She did not suffer terribly in the mornings, so neither did I. Nor did she yark even one time full-on, so neither did I. Couple of close calls, sure.

She is not cranky. The only true aggravation for her, exceptin for the rather cumbersome swelly of the belly, which of course I do not mind one bit and feel quite empathetic towards, is her allergies. She is one stopped up mouth breathing mess the second she lays down even sorta semi flat. Can't sleep and sneezes most moistly and violently about 60 times a day.

I bore you with this tedium because…

This morning we're driving to the doctor for an ultrasound, OK, and we're on the freeway flying along about 80 miles an hour like everybody else and Meg is sneezing mightily and as we take the exit in the dense frighteningly frenetic chaos that is LA traffic, she decides this would be a goodtime to take her vitties.

Her "Duet". Duet is a pre-natal vitamin pac that she's been almost religiously devoted to ever since the Walgreens incident.

Two yellow liquid gel caps that are just a skooch too big to go down easy. She pops one in just as an old VW Van almost ran smack into my hind-end, and I screamed…'Pay Attention Hippie!!'

That pill was about half way down her throat, chased by some fresh, cold pomegranate juice, when she started laughin.

'Oh no, it's stuck… it's gonna…'

Time warps into super slow-mo… she looks to me, beseechingly, her wide eyes filled with panic and dread…the nose, the red nose, pulled up and back all the way, twitching to and fro…

And I swear, seriously you guys, she sneezed so hard, that big yellow pill came flying right out her NOSE, it splatted damply off the windshield and fell right back onto her dress.

Sticky purple juice just sprayt erywhere!

Laws, children, I have never laughed so hard in my whole life and she ain't neither, she just almost gave herself a full on asthma attack.

She was about to take that pill again, the one that just flew out her nose, when I snatched it away from her and threw it out the window at the hippies.

Anybody remember that Johnny Cash song, "A Boy Named Sue"?

We are having a son.

Doc Phillips prophesies that he will be a very Big Boy. Shocking.

We saw his little face today, right thru Peg's belly, and his heart and his spine and his fingers and his toes...

I saw him. And I could crumble. And we saw his wiener. He he.

Cooper Jack Morris, he shall be called.

Not Wuby Thue.

Sorry bout that, dude.

Coming soon.

SMACK

2009

So there we are at the hospital on a perfectly good Monday nite here in Sunny So Cal. Simmer down, everybody's fine, no one ill nor injured. We are taking a baby class in a nearby hospital. A child parenting safety CPR LaMaze Circumspection Breastfeeding slowly drive your baby home and change his diaper class. A very smart looking young Pediatrician Dr. Woman all the way from Armenia was there and said she aimed to tell us what to expect. I asked her how many kids she had, and she said none.

So I snorted.

Right there on the front row, in plain view of

about forty pregnant people, Meg smacked me in the back of my head.

Hard.

'Disproportionate response to the offense,' I protest.

Right off, the Good Doctor asked how many of us intend to breastfeed and I raised my hand.

So Meg smacked me in the head again.

Harder.

I said, 'I think maybe I'll just go wait in the car.'

Meg said, 'Yes, please do.'

But I didn't.

The Good Doctor asked us what might be some of the benefits of Breastfeeding. One pregger said Bonding, another said Antibodies, and yet another thought it was much cheaper than buying formula. One pregger said it will help us lose the pregnancy

weight. Turns out all of these are true.
So I said... 'Uhm... Bigger Boobies?'

Seemed obvious to me.

The Good Doctor glared at me like I just shook the baby.

Silence.

Crickets.

Daggers.

Silence.

'I'm just saying, for Meg, not for me, but for Meg... being pregnant is first and foremostly about gittin her some big ole Boobies.

Smack.

LEGACY

2011

Today was my birthday, the best one ever. Meg hired a babysitter then scooped me up and took me out for an authentic Mexican dining experience, accompanied by a pitcher of icy Sangria. I don't imbibe very often, so I didn't really taste the alcohol till it made a rather rude and violent return some hours later. Meg only had a sip, then she drove us to the Hollywood Bowl for their July 4th Extravaganza! Vince Gill and the LA Phil, fireworks and everything. Super fun.

Hey fellas, did ya ever run into the bathroom right before the concert starts or the movie starts and ya don't really need to go, but she's going, so you figure ya might as well give it a shot? Anybody? I mean, who wants to stand out there all by himself?

Not me.

So I'm standing there at the urinal, as ya do, no privacy walls, just a bunch of men lined up like animals, wieners in the wind out there on public display... and not much is coming out of mine. I confess I'm a little light-headed and short-winded from the walk up that hill, and assuming that this will be my last chance for a while... I hold my breath and give it that one big final push, to ya know, get it all out.

Laws, I feels dizzy...

Next thing I know, my legs kinda noodle and I'm slowly falling forward, not quite asleep, but just almost.

I look up in time to see that the wall, which my forehead is about to smack, it's got a big nasty booger on it, right above where my left eyebrow will surely land. Excuse my vulgarity, but what kinda person stands at the urinal picking his nose and just flicks it on the wall?

You do see it everywhere tho, even in fancy

restaurants and opera houses. I bet you girls didn't know that. Boys are gross. And I'll tell ya something else for free... men, grown men, that teach our children and invest our money and preach in our churches and cure what ails us, these same men whilst in the public toilet will just fart out loud standing right there not two feet from a total stranger. An older gentleman, say, late sixties and up, he won't care AT ALL. He will look you in your face and just fart out loud. It makes me giggle every time, cuz what can you do, really?

Not a thing, just stand there and take it.

My mind shouts at my body... 'Oohh Nooo, Adjust! Right the Ship, reverse engines, stand up straight!' Time slows, I close my eyes, and I face-plant right into that stucco wall and the aforementioned booger above said urinal. This hurts my nose and my feelings, but my unresponsive arms have rebelliously remained at waist level and are now pinned under me. It's all my legs can do to keep me in the upright and locked position. Suddenly, I feel the chill of cold water, for in the fall I seem to have flushed the toilet with my very chin. After a super long helpless few seconds, I did push back against my forehead and that folks, is when the trickle of blood began to flow. Stucco is hard and pointy.

What, this never happened to any of you?

My shorts and my belly are sopping wet, and I glance at the hippie next to me and nod... 'what's up? I'm ok. It's my birthday.'

Now what? Mildly intoximacated and soaking wet in the Hollywood Bowl at such a Patriotic event.

I try to compose myself. Did I just pass out in a nasty, public toilet? Walking slowly and with focused determination I'm gonna wash my hands and draw up a plan. Dry myself off. I'm pretty sure I only had three, maybe four glasses of that Hawaiian Punch, I can totally pull myself together, right?

Meg's gonna kill me. I start rubbing my hands together under the nozzle, but no water flows. I wave my hands back and forth, vigorously, what is wrong with this stupid thing? Of course I get the only one that doesn't work. The hippie, anxiously awaiting my encore, says... 'Ya gotta push that button on the end, the one that says "push".'

'Oh, yeah. Thanks,' says I.

There are no paper towels. Oh wait, yes there are, there's a big wad of them down there on the floor, trumpled on and dirty. I go to meet Meg under the tree as instructed, and as I approach, she glares all agape and agah at me and asks...

What have you done?

What dya mean?

Your shirt is wet and sticking to your stomach in a very unflattering way.

You don't like it?

Not your best look.

Yeah.

Your fly is down.

Oops. I can fix that.

Why is your nose bleeding?

I'm not bleeding.

Why is your forehead bleeding?

I might have slipped.

In a public toilet?

I didn't mean to.

So this is pee all over your clothes?

No, not really, it's just toilet water.

Oh good, I was afraid you might stink all nite.

Yeah.

What's that in your eyebrow?

I didn't throw up or nothing.

You smell like you did.

You can't smell me.

Look at me! Stop waving at people like you're the village idiot or something.

Yeah.

What is that?

Stop! Don't touch it. It's a booger.

Of course it is. Is it yours?

Nope.

Jay Hunter, whose booger do you have on your face?

I don't know.

You are so gross right now.

There were no paper towels!

Why don't you just wipe it on your shirt?

Give me a heiny wipe.

Now I have to carry a diaper bag when I go out with you?

Yeah.

Did you go ahead and poop your pants while you were in there?

Yeah.

Now you're trying to sound like Rain Man?

Yeah.

Stop it.

Gotta go to K-Mart.

Who's that Hippie pointing at us?

Just some guy I met inside.

Why are they laughing?

Maybe because I fell in the toilet?

That's probably it.

Probably.

Well Happy Birthday Mr. Booger Head, you're famous!

Thanks.

That's some legacy you're leaving our

Son.

Yeah.

ZIGGY

2011

April 25, 2011

It's 4:20 pm, I am laying on the Stage at the San Francisco Opera, and on just the other side of that dilapidated trailer lies my fate. The powers that be are discussing me and the notion that I might sing the title role in *Siegfried*, right here right now at one of the super coolest Opera Companies in the whole wide world. You Opera geeks out there know the significance and magnitude of such an opportunity, and you also know that Ziggy, as I like to think of him, is one of the greatest challenges to any tenors' throat, psyche, and sphincter.

It's just super scary long and hard.

There's a big red clock on the wall up there staring me right in the face and it seems to be creeping along, taunting me, no rush, nothing at stake here. Twenty-seven minutes later, they offer me a handshake, some love, and what is without a doubt a once in a lifetime chance.

I can do this.

PS...

May 25, 2011

SFO's *Notes from Valhalla*

Okay, so I'm going to sing young Siegfried. In San Francisco, in Francesca Zambello's New Production. YIKES! Maybe some of you out there wanna know what that feels like? You think you want a peek behind this curtain? I'll try and explain.

First of all, this is HARD! Don't let anybody tell ya different.

There's an enormous bucket of notes and pitches and words and dynamics and phrases and umlauts and long vowels and double consonants and unstressed syllables and vocal stylings that must all receive their due diligence in this almost five hour long opera. Stage left, sit here, hammer a sword, spank the bear, up on the trailer, head out the window, down on your knees, kiss the girl, break the spear, pull his ear, kick the bucket but don't drink the poison, sing pretty but don't push, do slay the dragon but please, watch the conductor. What's he singing and where's she going, don't scream in her ear but don't sing upstage, don't spray em with spit, be a nice colleague and how's my German and how's my breath, and that's gotta be the 1,000th high note I've sung today… and the Tarnhelm is a what? Keeping it all straight is not easy. Not for me anyway.

So right off the bat that all adds up to one very large serving of sheer terror. Can I do this? Can I get it right? Breathe deep, nice and slow, go to your happy place.

Second off… this is FUN. Tomorrow I am going to be a sixteen-year-old fearless, naïve, horn tootin', super-strong, fireproof hero that understands the birds and the beasts. And I will sing some of the most gorgeous and challenging music ever written! I am surrounded by brilliant musicians who are lending their years of experience and support and gentle reminders and pages of notes and suggestions, all in the spirit of molding me into my finest Siegfried. That feels really good.

Now, I promise you, it is a very long way from my childhood home in Paris, Texas, to this stage in San Francisco. That is more often than not, my greatest source of fear —

country boy that I am — taking on Siegfried. For all the world to see.

But it's time to put that nonsense behind me and enjoy every minute. I'm gonna do my homework, and get my sleep and eat my fruits and veggies and I'm going to be prepared to do my very best every time the music starts. Each day I'm getting a little stronger, a little more confident, finding my groove, so I slap those doubting demons off my shoulder and count my blessings and say, Yes I can! I can do this.

I can do this.

TING DRAGON

2012

Several years ago, in the Intro to my website I wrote these words…

I've learned that for me, there probably won't be some big break, some new production or role or voice lesson or coaching that just brings it all together and everything will suddenly just click, and I'll be a great tenor and in great demand and will possess a flawless technique and I will behave properly and have panache and be clever and artsy and thin and everyone will love me. Not likely. For most of us that just doesn't happen. I just have to do the work. No shortcuts. I have to study hard and practice wisely and passionately, and I should find a very smart agent and let her do all the talking.

I was wrong. Well, about some of it. I'm still not very artsy or thin nor terribly clever. I cannot seem to muster much panache. My technique, all these years later is still far from flawless. But that part about getting or not getting a big break, that needs a little updating.

I got a big break all right. First in San Francisco, and if that weren't enough, now here in New York City. In the World of Classical Music this simply must be considered the single greatest opportunity a singer can receive. Just last Saturday, I sang Siegfried in *Siegfried*, in a new production at The Metropolitan Opera. It was broadcast Live in HD into movie theaters the whole world over.

That's pretty much the operatic equivalent of the World Series, the Super Bowl, the World Cup, the very Tour de France.

Now, lest you should worry that I might get too big for my britches, let me offer that I have given but seven performances of Ziggy. Which surely puts me dead last in the world standings. Neither has my journey been any more difficult or compelling than anyone else's. We all have to work hard, I bet you every single person who has ever sung on that stage at some time or another waited tables or drove trucks or shoed horses or sold panties or repaired cars or delivered pizzas to pay their way. Me too. But I've always had an inkling that if I'd keep practicing, just keep getting better, that one fine day my throat would obey me. And I'd get to keep singing. And that my friend, is the very best part of this big break; I'm gonna get to keep zingin.

My son Cooper Jack is just two and a half years old and I don't reckon he'll remember much about all this. He did yell "Daddy Ting Dragon" over and over at the top of his lungs for a couple of weeks there. He might be curious some day about how his very own father got to sing that role on that stage, and what it felt like. And tho I do feel inclined to impart details of these marvelous times, I must also give warning - you cynical, sneering, naysayer types best turn back. It's gonna get warm and fuzzy in here.

Someday he might like to know that I have been pursuing this Operatic singing career for twenty-three years now and I have had a ball! I have sung all kinds of music all over this planet and there really have not been more than a handful of dull moments. I've known lots of feast and lots of famine. I've had plenty and I've been flat broke, 40 years old, staying with my Momma in Paris, Texas. I'd like Cooper to know that the hard times weren't that bad, I was never too blue, and they lend a uniquely delicious seasoning to these most fabulous of days.

But let's back up a little. Over the last six years my singing career took a slow dive into a professional funk. A valley. I couldn't get hired. Stuff here and there, sure, supporting roles, understudies, but my phone was quickly learning not to ring. That's hard on a person. Every singer out there dreads that inevitable day when no one on this Earth will pay him to sing. At one such fragile moment, Speight Jenkins offered me a job covering Ziggy in Seattle. I accepted, not because I thought I could zing it, or because I was re-inventing myself as a heldentenor or any of that nonsense, I simply had no choice, no options, it was the only card on the table. And we had us a baby on the way, so I said 'yes please, thank you.'

After about six months of intense study I began to fully grasp the enormity of and outright impossibility of ever learning, much less memorizing this part. Siegfried appears in the last two operas of Wagner's *Ring* cycle, and he sings about a gazillion words and not one of them is easy. Every day my eyes grew wider and my stomach more acidic and my self-confidence was nowhere to be found and I saw absolutely nothing good ever coming out of this. One afternoon in the Burbank Library I'm pretty sure I swooned. I wanted to quit, I wanted out, I know it's not mortal combat or brain surgery, but still, I did not want to study that music for one more day!

Every nite I prayed "Lordy, Please, Let this cup pass from me! Please!"

But He didn't.

I'm pretty sure he said "If you'll quit yer whining, I've got a little something in mind."

So I learned it and I was second string Siegfried in Seattle and LA and I started off that way in San Francisco too. Even the Metropolitan Opera hired me to be their understudy, probably because there are so few of us out there that know it.

My friend and fellow tenor Gary Lehman was to sing it in this new production at the Met, but he got sick and had to withdraw. I know it broke his heart, and he didn't deserve that.

Seriously you guys, I would have bet the farm that Peter Gelb would choose to bring in a big star or someone who's had lots of experience in the role, but he didn't. He did not know me at all when he asked me, with only two rehearsals left before the opening.... 'Can you really do this?'

I didn't blink and said, 'Yes, I can.'

So he gave me a shot. Told me to do my best.

At this point, I must tip my proverbial hat to the multitude of gifted, talented singers and artists and players out there who never get a chance to perform that plum role on a great stage. We work and we study and we take classes and lessons and we coach and exercise and practice and go to THERAPY and we wait. And we wait. We all require an unending supply of Good Fortune and Good Timing to stay afloat in the entertainment biz, and I have, quite obviously, been immeasurably blessed with both. We all need that golden opportunity. And this time, Hallelujah, This Time Around, I am ready! Can I get an Amen!?

Someday Cooper might want to know what it felt like…to get the biggest of all big breaks. I'm sorry son, I don't remember. You and your Momma were here in the city with me in a studio apartment and it was cold and snowing and I couldn't sleep and y'all couldn't sleep and there was this enormous Siegfried poster out in front of the Met that I walked by everyday and the adrenaline was using my body as a punching bag and next thing ya know I'm on that stage trying to be seventeen and what's my blocking and cameras everywhere and oh, nice to meet you Maestro, and goodness this is slippery and then all of a sudden I'm singing with Bryn Terfel and Deborah Voigt and just listen to that orchestra and it's gonna be broadcast to how many countries? Me? In the hardest role, like, ever? At the Met?

No wonder it was all a blur. My only moments of clarity were those onstage once the performance began. Thank goodness, there was calm in the eye of that storm, and I disappeared into the music and the story for those few hours. I felt just almost fearless.

And I wish this for my boy... someday I hope you get to face something so much bigger than you, something way too hard, way too scary, and I hope you get to look your fear in the face, and stand your ground.

Because it feels so good.

No matter what anybody else says or thinks, I know I did my best.

And I know you will too.

I have no idea how this will play out, if this is the beginning of a new, even better chapter or the apex of a long and slow, steady climb.

But I've got a good feeling about this.

I'll let ya know,

JMo

ABOUT THE AUTHOR

Photo Credit Vii Tanner

AS SIEGFRIED AT THE METROPOLITAN OPERA:

"It's the understudy's job to save the show, and that's just what Jay Hunter Morris did Thursday at the Met in the daunting title role of Wagner's *Siegfried*. ... Morris brandished a bright, lyric voice that pierced Wagner's massive orchestrations. Tall, blond and broad-shouldered, the tenor — who started on Broadway in 1995's *Master Class* — even looked the part of a Teutonic dragon slayer." (James Jorden, New York Post, October 28, 2011)

AS CAPTAIN AHAB AT THE SAN FRANCISCO OPERA:

"Jay Hunter Morris's Ahab is a "Force of Nature" at San Francisco Opera. Here's the top take-away from *Moby-Dick* : the power of tenor Jay Hunter Morris as Ahab, peg-legged commander of the good ship Pequod, spouting his words like water from the blowhole of a whale. At Wednesday's opening performance, in this adaptation of Herman Melville's epic novel, he sang with a pressurized fury that practically shook the seats of the War Memorial Opera House. Think Old Testament. Think King Lear. Amazing Morris stepped on stage and announced Ahab's obsession, his will to capture and kill the great white whale: "Infinity! Infinity! We will harvest infinity!" (Richard Scheinin, San Jose Mercury News, October 11, 2011)

AS CAPTAIN AHAB: STATE OPERA OF SOUTH AUSTRALIA

"Jay Hunter Morris was simply magnificent as Ahab in a very demanding heldentenor role. We have come to expect excellence from him following his superb performances for Opera Australia as Pinkerton in the 1990's and as Erik in *The Flying Dutchman* more recently. His initial Otello-like appearance with ringing top notes sung over an expanded chorus set the scene for a finely judged performance both vocally and dramatically. Every nuance was extracted from his role with alternating scenes of fiery outbursts, contemplative soliloquy, crazed passion and his final descent into complete madness with a crazed look in his eye. The tall blond and youthful Texan looked unrecognizable as a much older, craggy sea salt with a peg leg." (Opera Australia Insider, September 11, 2011)

READ JAY HUNTER MORRIS' DELIGHTFUL INTERVIEW WITH
WWW.OPERALIVELY.COM

From the home page, look at the widget on the top left corner, click on Exclusive Interviews, and scroll down the list of names to click on Jay's.